Printable Versions available on Etsy
www.etsy.com/shop/TriggMo

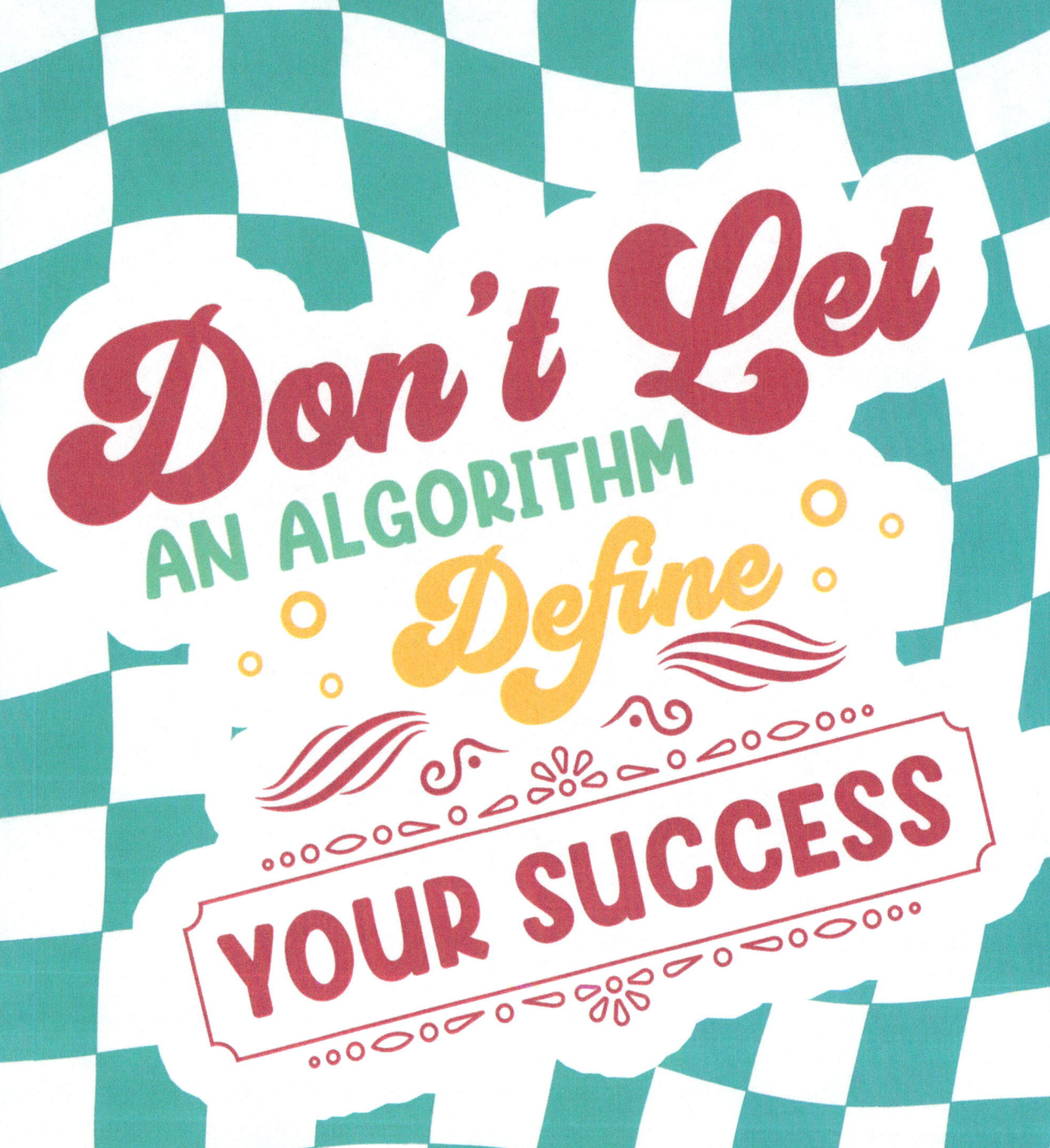

A Note Just for You

Java Jolt Needed

RUNNING ON FUMES? GET A CAFFEINE ZOOM!

FOR YOUR CAFFEINE FIX

Cafeteria Conundrum

TIRED OF MYSTERY MEAT?

SAVE YOUR SANITY!

FOR REAL FOOD ADVENTURES

Sweet Tooth Solution

Life's too short, eat dessert first!

For your sweet treats

Pizza Emergency

PIZZA IS LIFE.

NEED I SAY MORE?

FOR YOUR PIZZA CRAVINGS

Take Your Dreams SERIOUSLY

Feeling Fuzzy?

SNiFFLES GOT YOU DOWN?

FIGHT BACK!

FOR YOUR HEALTH NEEDS

Gasoline Gloom

EMPTY TANK?

DON'T LET IT CRANK!

FOR YOUR GAS NEEDS

It's Okay
To Not
Be Okay

Outfit Upgrade

OUT OF STYLE? TIME FOR A PILE!

FOR A NEW OUTFIT

Movie Night Magic

BORED? MOVIE NIGHT TO THE RESCUE!

FOR MOVIE NIGHT FUN

MINDSET

IS WHAT *Separates* THE BEST FROM THE REST

POSITIVE *mind* POSITIVE *vibes* POSITIVE *lives*

Book Boost

NEED A READ? FEED YOUR BRAIN INDEED!

FOR YOUR NEXT READ

Pamper Patrol

STRESSED? PAMPER YOURSELF!

FOR A LITTLE PAMPERING

Munchies Madness

HUNGRY? SNACK ATTACK!

FOR YOUR SNACK STASH

Study Break Bliss

BRAIN FRIED? TIME TO UNWIND!

FOR YOUR STUDY BREAKS

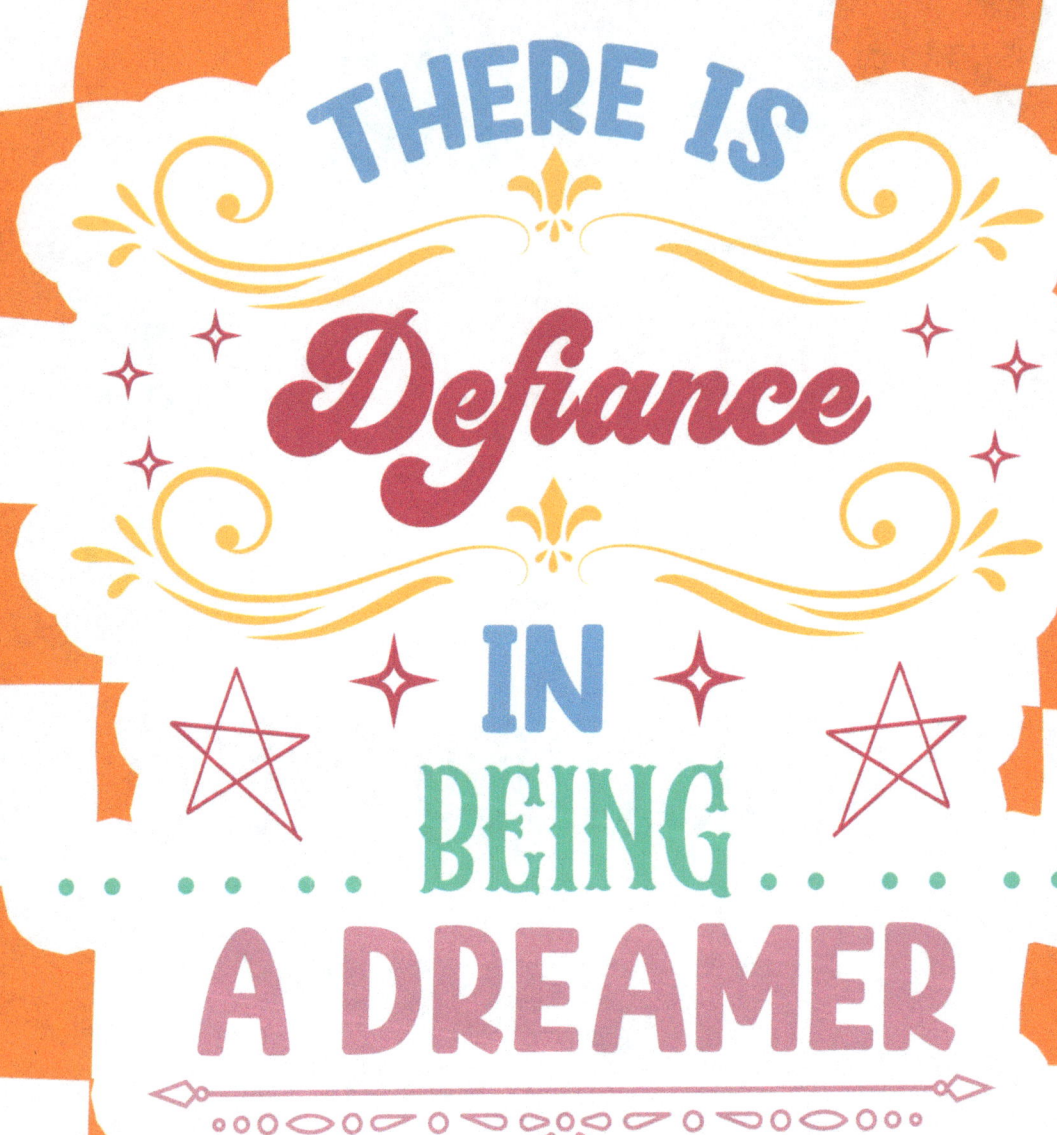

THERE IS *Defiance* IN BEING A DREAMER

Road Trip Ready

ADVENTURE AWAITS? LET'S HIT THE ROAD!

FOR ROAD TRIP ESSENTIALS

You Deserve the Love You keep trying to give everyone else

Call Home Comfort

MISS HOME? MAKE THE CALL!

FOR CALLING HOME

A Note
Just for You

The world is a
Better
place
with you in it

Ride Rescue

STRANDED?

HITCH A RIDE!

FOR WHEN YOU NEED A RIDE

Study Support

NEED HELP?

TUTORS ARE YOUR FRIENDS!

FOR STUDY HELP

A Note
Just for You

Music Magic

BORED OF SILENCE? TUNE IN!

FOR NEW MUSIC

Supply Savvy

Out of pens?

Time to make amends!

For school supply surprises

You are
Capable
of amazing
things

Laundry Lifesaver

DIRTY CLOTHES? TIME TO FOLD!

FOR LAUNDRY SUPPLIES

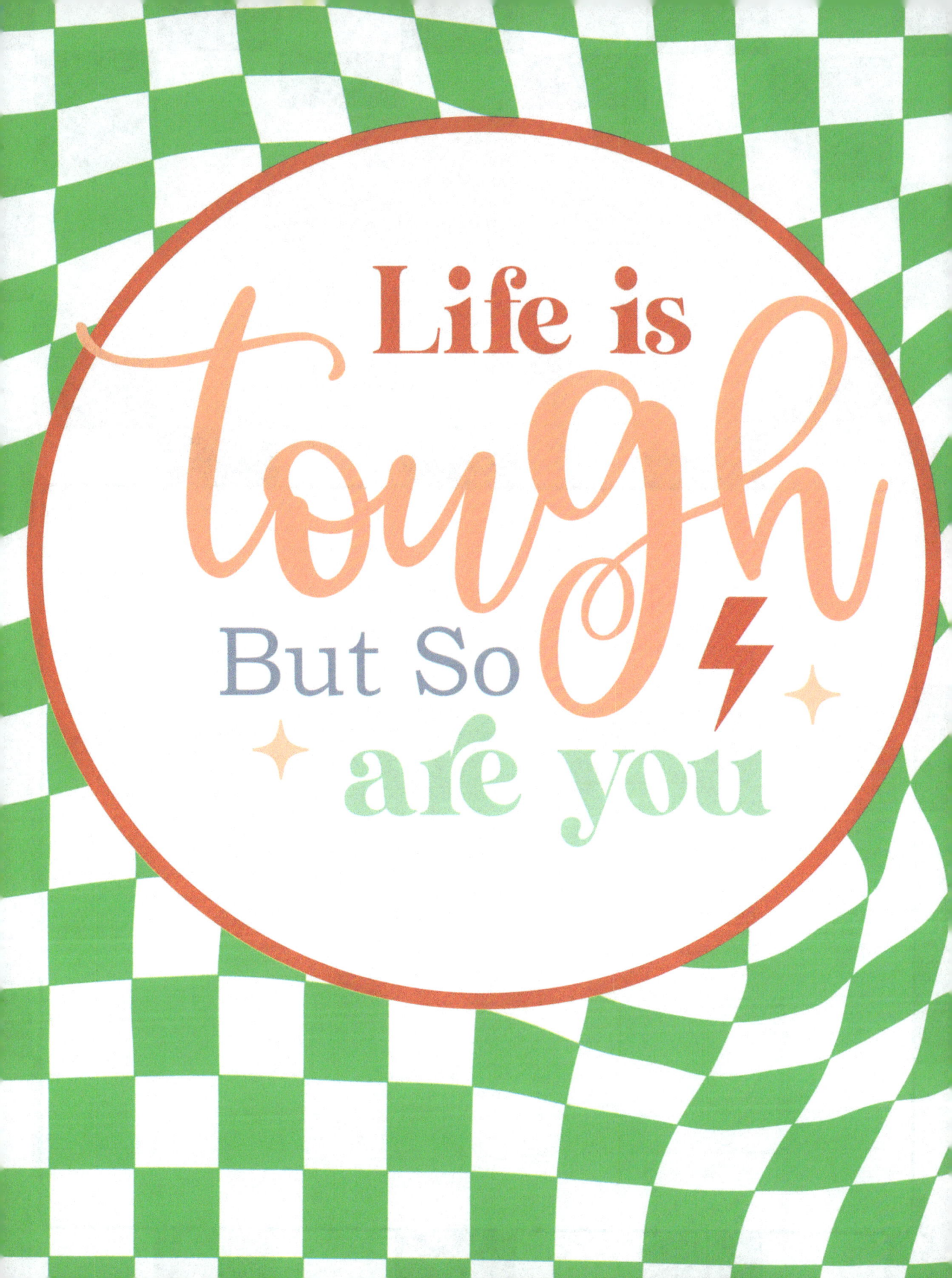

Delivery Delight

HUNGRY? DELIVERY TO THE RESCUE!

FOR FOOD DELIVERED TO YOU

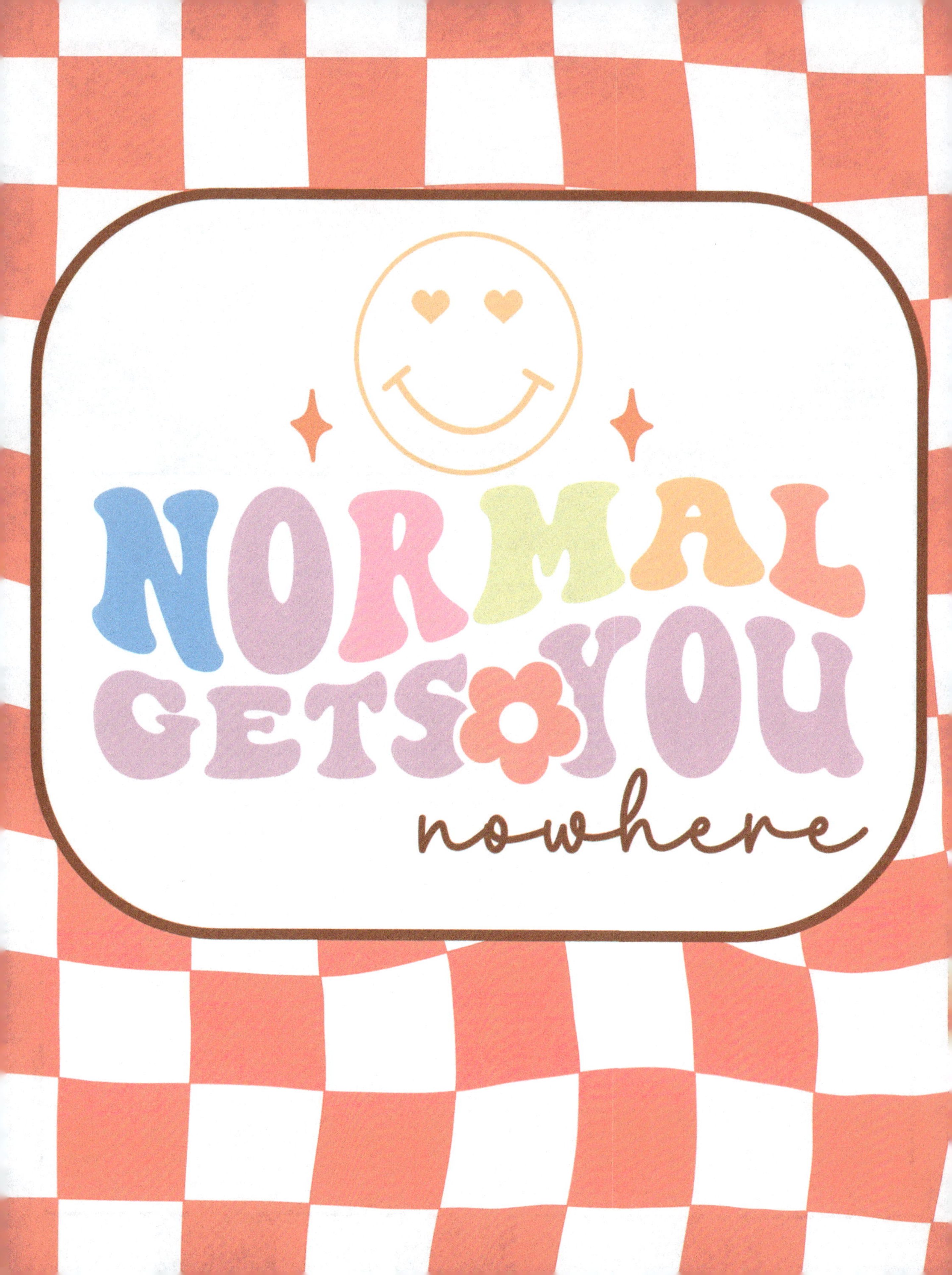
NORMAL
GETS YOU
nowhere

Room Revamp

DULL ROOM?

LET'S GET CREATIVE!

FOR ROOM ESSENTIALS

Made in the USA
Columbia, SC
10 April 2025

56399657R10043